I am *NOT* an Idiot!

Written and Illustrated by: Jeff Amster

Copyright © 2016 by Jeff Amster. All rights reserved.

This book or any text within it may not be reproduced or used in any manner whatsoever except for the use of brief quotations in a scholarly work or book review. Any other uses requires express written permission by the author. For permissions or further information, contact jeff.amster@gmail.com.

Written and Illustrated by Jeff Amster

Edited by Jeff Amster and Melissa Amster

First Printing, 2016

ISBN 978-0-692-77843-2

Ordering information: Special discounts are available for quantity purchases by bookstores, corporations, associations and others. For details, contact jeff.amster@gmail.com

To my wonderful wife, Melissa, my muse and best friend...

To our amazing children - E.Z., M.A., and M.P.

I am fortunate that as a family we inspire each other to be the best people we can be (and laugh in the process)...

When it's hot out and we're rushing to get inside, don't yell at me as I unlock the door - I know the right key to use and how to open a door.

You may be uncomfortable **BUT...**

I am **NOT** an idiot!

When I'm playing during screen time, you ask me to turn it off but I am almost done with a hard level - I know how to shut it off.

It may be annoying for you
BUT...

I am NOT an idiot!

Sometimes, I change my mind for what I want to eat or drink for dinner even after I've told you I really wanted something else.

It may be frustrating for you BUT...

I am **NOT** an idiot!

When it's bath time and I take an extra long time playing when I need to finish washing my hair - I know how making hair bubbles works!

It may be grueling for you

BUT...

I am **NOT** an idiot!

BUT...When I am out and see other people that don't look like me, and I make silly voices to make my brother and sister laugh...

Teach me about other cultures **BECAUSE...**

I am **BEING** an idiot!

AND...When I see a man who needs help, and I say he should just get a job to buy food and a home since it's easy...

Teach me about compassion **BECAUSE...**

I am **BEING** an idiot!

AND...When I toss garbage on the ground because it's quick, even when recycling bins are just a few steps away...

Teach me about conservation
BECAUSE...

I am **BEING** an idiot!

Though I love to do everything right away and by myself, I need to also love and care about the people and situations around me.

By treating everyone with *RESPECT...*

We

are

NOT

idiots!

www.ingramcontent.com/pod-product-compliance
Lightning Source LLC
Chambersburg PA
CBHW042146290426
44110CB00002B/127